I0606251

BLASTOFF! READERS, AN IMPRINT OF BELLWETHER MEDIA BY FLUTTERBEE

Blastoff! Readers are carefully developed by literacy experts to build reading stamina and move students toward fluency by combining standards-based content with developmentally appropriate text.

LEVELS

Level 1 provides the most support through repetition of high-frequency words, light text, predictable sentence patterns, and strong visual support.

Level 2 offers early readers a bit more challenge through varied sentences, increased text load, and text-supportive special features.

Level 3 advances early-fluent readers toward fluency through increased text load, less reliance on photos, advancing concepts, longer sentences, and more complex special features.

★ **Blastoff! Universe**

Reading Level

Grade
K

Grades
1–3

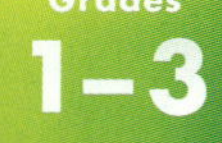

Grade
4

This edition first published in 2026 by Bellwether Media, Inc.

For information regarding permission, write to Bellwether Media, Inc., Attention: Permissions Department, 3500 American Blvd W, Suite 150, Bloomington, MN 55431.

Library of Congress Cataloging-in-Publication Data is available at www.loc.gov or upon request from the publisher.

ISBN: 9798893047905 (hardcover)
ISBN: 9798893048902 (ebook)

Editor: Elizabeth Neuenfeldt   Designer: Brittany McIntosh

Printed in the United States of America, North Mankato, MN.

Table of Contents

What Are Capybaras?

Capybaras are **mammals**. They are the world's biggest **rodents**! They mostly live in South America. Many live in the Amazon **rainforest**.

Greater Capybara Report

range =

Status in the Wild

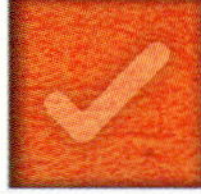

least concern

Habitats

rainforests

savannas

wetlands

Capybaras grow to be about 2 feet (0.6 meters) tall.

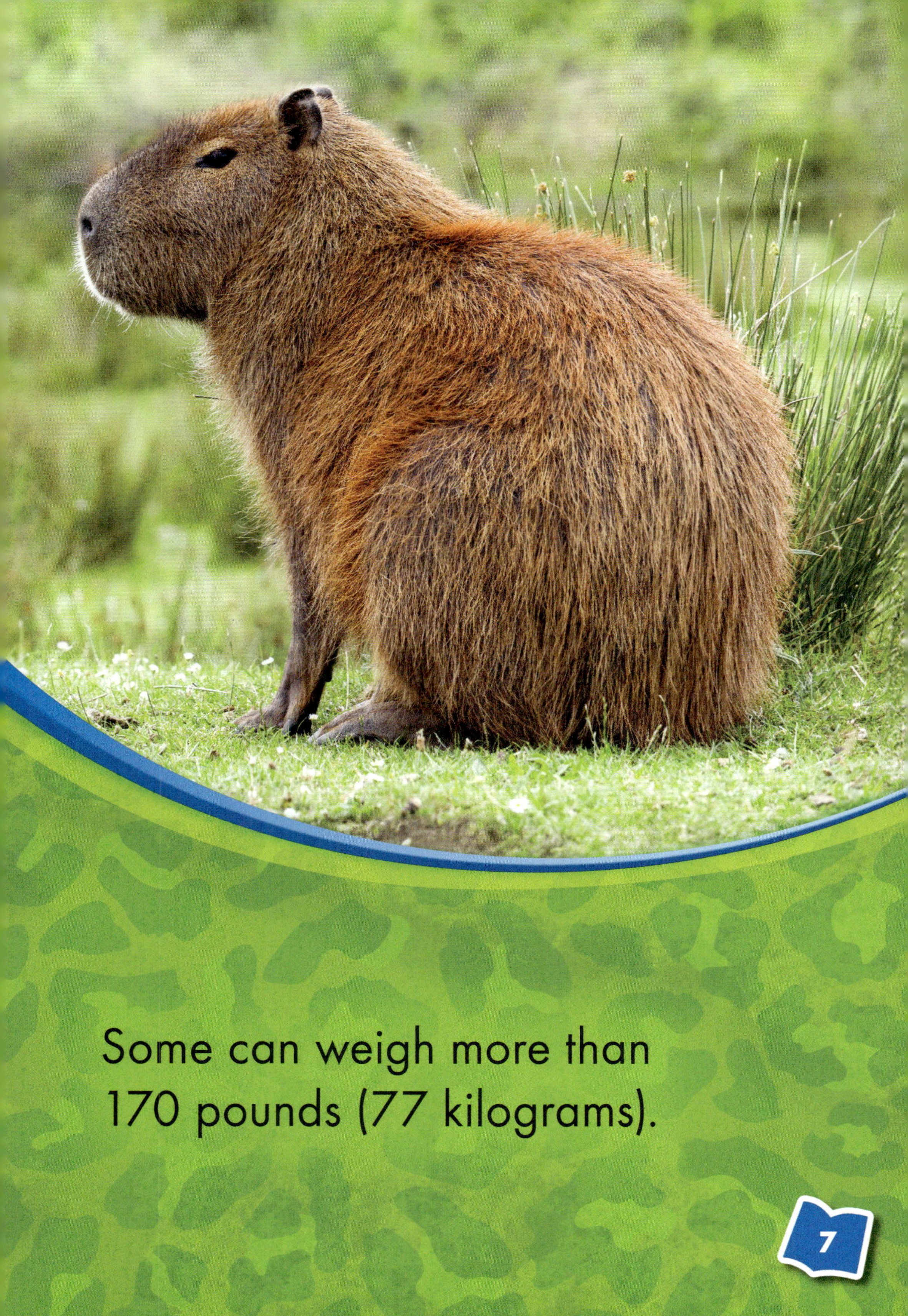

Some can weigh more than
170 pounds (77 kilograms).

Capybaras have dark brown or reddish-brown fur. Their fur is rough.

Capybaras have **webbed feet**. These help capybaras swim.

Capybaras have big and sharp front teeth.

Their eyes, ears, and noses are near the tops of their heads. This helps them watch for **predators** while they swim.

Spot a Capybara
big and sharp front teeth
dark brown or reddish-brown fur
webbed feet

Life by the Water

Capybaras live in rainforests, **savannas**, and **wetlands**. Most live in groups to stay safe.

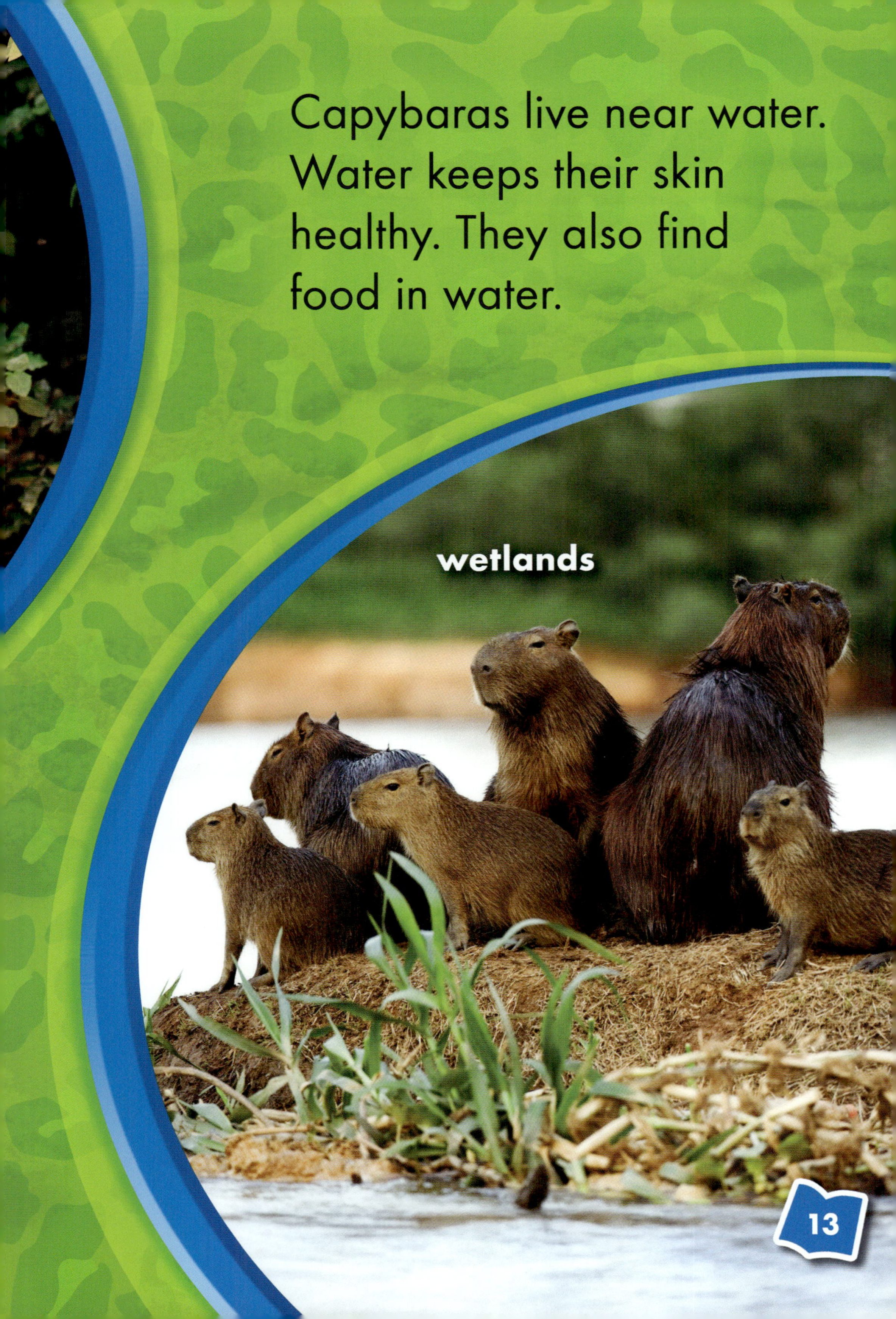

Capybaras live near water. Water keeps their skin healthy. They also find food in water.

These rodents are most active at sunrise and sunset.

They swim underwater to avoid predators. They can stay underwater for five minutes!

Capybaras are **herbivores**.
They eat **sedges** and grasses.

They also eat their own poop. This helps them **digest** their food.

Growing Up

Female capybaras give birth to up to eight **pups**. This happens once a year.

Pups drink mom's milk. They can walk soon after birth.

Capybara pups begin to eat grasses after one week. They stay with mom for about a year.

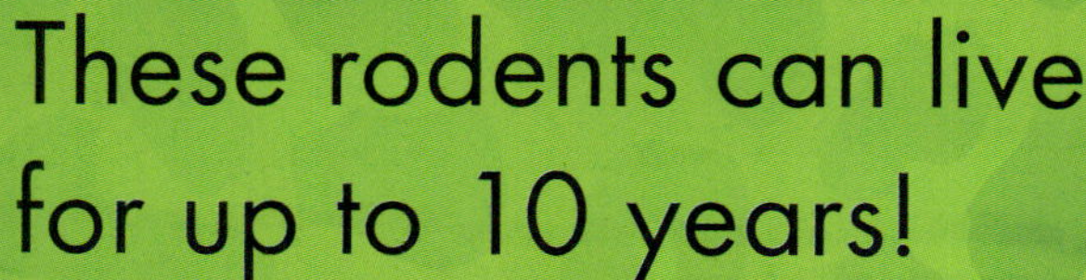

These rodents can live for up to 10 years!

Life of a Capybara

Name of Babies

pups

Number of Babies

up to 8

Time Spent with Mom

about 1 year

Life Span

Glossary

digest—to break down food

herbivores—animals that only eat plants

mammals—warm-blooded animals that have backbones and feed their young milk

predators—animals that hunt other animals for food

pups—baby capybaras

rainforest—a thick, green forest that receives a lot of rain

rodents—small mammals that gnaw on their food; mice, rats, and squirrels are all rodents.

savannas—flat grasslands with few trees

sedges—grassy plants that grow in wet areas

webbed feet—feet that have skin connecting the toes

wetlands—areas of land that are covered with low levels of water for most of the year

To Learn More

AT THE LIBRARY

Brody, Walt. *Capybaras: Nature's Biggest Rodent.* Minneapolis, Minn.: Lerner Publications, 2024.

Mata, Julia. *Capybara: A First Field Guide to the Biggest Rodent in the World.* London, U.K.: Neon Squid, 2024.

Pang, Ursula. *Capybaras.* Buffalo, N.Y.: PowerKids Press, 2025.

ON THE WEB

FACTSURFER

Factsurfer.com gives you a safe, fun way to find more information.

1. Go to www.factsurfer.com.
2. Enter "capybaras" into the search box and click 🔍.
3. Select your book cover to see a list of related content.

Index

The images in this book are reproduced through the courtesy of: Steph Mattioli, front cover (capybara); MatteoFar8, front cover (background), pp. 2-3; moskha.com, p. 3; imageBROKER.com/ Alamy Stock Photo, p. 4; Kevin Xu Photography, p. 6; Anneka, p. 7; PhotocechCZ, p. 8; mlharing, p. 9 (top); Kevin Schafer/ Alamy Stock Photo, p. 9 (bottom); donna Ikenberry/ Art Directors/ Alamy Stock Photo, p. 10; Wirestock Creators, pp. 10-11; scottnguyen, p. 11; imageBROKER.com GmbH & Co. KG/ Alamy Stock Photo, p. 12; Panoramic Images/ Alamy Stock Photo, p. 13; Danita Delimont/ Alamy Stock Photo, p. 14; Giedriius, pp. 15, 18-19; Carolina Jaramillo, pp. 16-17; Bildagentur Zoonar GmbH, p. 17 (jaguars); Ondrej Prosicky, p. 17 (pumas); FotoRequest, p. 17 (caimans); loremipsumdasilva, p. 17 (capybara); piemags/ nature/ Alamy Stock Photo, p. 17 (sedges, grasses); Thomas Faull, p. 18; Janet Horton/ Alamy Stock Photo, p. 20; Laura Romin & Larry Dalton/ Alamy Stock Photo, p. 21; Henner Damke, p. 23.